TOP 10 PROFESSIONAL FOOTBALL COACHES

Jeff Savage

SPORTS TOP 10

Enslow Publishers, Inc.

44 Fadem Road   PO Box 38
Box 699   Aldershot
Springfield, NJ 07081   Hants GU12 6BP
USA   UK

Library of Congress Cataloging-in-Publication Data

Savage, Jeff.
    Top 10 professional football coaches / Jeff Savage.
       p. cm. — (Sports top 10)
    Includes bibliographical references (p.) and index.
    Summary: Profiles the lives and careers of Paul Brown, Joe Gibbs, Bud
Grant, George Halas, Jimmy Johnson, Curly Lambeau, Tom Landry, Vince
Lombardi, Don Shula, and Bill Walsh.
    ISBN 0-7660-1006-6
    1. Football coaches—United States—Biography—Juvenile literature.
2. Football coaches—Rating of—United States—Juvenile literature. [1. Football
coaches.] I. Title. II. Series.
GV939.A1S26 1998
796.332'64'092273—dc21
[B]   97-20381
                                              CIP
                                              AC

Printed in the United States of America

10 9 8 7 6 5 4 3 2 1

Illustration Credits: Chicago Bears, pp. 19, 21; Cincinnati Bengals, pp. 6,
9; © NFL Photos, pp. 34, 37; Dallas Cowboys Weekly, pp. 30, 33; Green Bay
Packers, pp. 27, 29; Jim Turner/NFL Photos, p. 43; Miami Dolphins, pp. 23,
25, 38, 41; Michael Zagaris/NFL Photos, p. 45; Minnesota Vikings, pp. 15,
17; Washington Redskins, pp. 10, 13.

Cover Illustration: Miami Dolphins

Interior Design: Richard Stalzer

CONTENTS

Introduction

HOW IMPORTANT IS A FOOTBALL COACH? Some people think that the players in the pads and helmets are the ones making the plays, while the coach just stands there. The truth is, the head coach does more for the team than anyone else. Here are some of the things that the head coach does:

The head coach must assemble a coaching staff. Coaches must choose a team of assistants who will understand their coaching methods and teach them to the players. All of the coaches must work well together.

The head coach must help build a team of players. The head coach must be able to recognize talent and decide which players best fit the needs of the team. NFL coaches must help recruit players from college, and make trades for them with other NFL teams.

The coach must be able to teach the players his or her system. On offense, the coach may design a ball-control running game, or a wide-open passing attack. On defense, the coach may prefer an aggressive man-to-man system or a zone scheme. Whatever the coach chooses, the coach then must put it down in a playbook and get the players to understand it.

The coach must study the opponent. Coaches must spend countless hours watching game films, sometimes staying up all night if they have to, looking for any weaknesses their opponents may have. Then they must design a game plan to combat their opponent.

In the game, head coaches must make the important decisions. They must decide whether to punt or go for it on fourth down, whether to try for a touchdown or settle for a field goal, whether to call time-out or let the clock run.

They may listen to advice from their assistants and players, but they have the final word.

Finally, coaches must win. They are the ones ultimately responsible for their team's performance. If their team wins, coaches playfully get a bucket of water dumped on them on the sideline; if the team begins to lose, the coach gets fired. Currently there are only thirty NFL head coaches at any one time. It is not easy to become one. It is even harder to stay one.

It is also hard to pick ten coaches and say they are the best ever. Hundreds of coaches have enjoyed success in the NFL. But the ten coaches we have chosen have left their mark on professional football.

CAREER STATISTICS

Coach	Years	Teams	Wins	Losses	Ties	Pct.
PAUL BROWN*	25	Browns, Bengals	213	104	9	.667
JOE GIBBS	12	Redskins	124	60	0	.674
BUD GRANT	18	Vikings	158	96	5	.620
GEORGE HALAS	40	Bears	313	148	32	.667
JIMMY JOHNSON	7	Cowboys, Dolphins	61	51	0	.545
CURLY LAMBEAU	33	Packers, Cardinals, Redskins	223	130	21	.624
TOM LANDRY	29	Cowboys	250	162	6	.605
VINCE LOMBARDI	10	Packers, Redskins	96	34	6	.728
DON SHULA	31	Colts, Dolphins	328	156	6	.676
BILL WALSH	10	49ers	92	59	1	.609

*Includes All-America Football Conference
**Statistics only include regular season totals.

PAUL BROWN

Paul Brown led his Cleveland teams to seven league championships, 4 in the AAFC, and 3 in the NFL.

PAUL BROWN

THE CLEVELAND BROWNS WERE WEAVING MAGIC once again. Coach Paul Brown was calling plays from the sideline and sending them in with messenger guards. It was the 1950 NFL season opener, with Brown's team matched against the defending champion Philadelphia Eagles.

Cleveland had just joined the NFL. The Browns were part of the smaller All-America Football Conference (AAFC), which had merged that year with the powerful National Football League. Cleveland had won the AAFC title all four years of its existence, compiling an amazing record of 47–4–3. But most people thought Brown's team would be swallowed up by the powerful NFL. That did not happen. With Brown relaying his plays to quarterback Otto Graham, the Browns surprised the Eagles, 35–10. "The score could have been much greater," said stunned Eagles tackle Bucko Kilroy. "It could have been 61–10."[1]

Brown used his unique messenger system to guide the Browns clear to the NFL championship game. In that game, Cleveland beat the Los Angeles Rams, 30–28, to win the title.

Cleveland's emergence in the NFL should have surprised no one. Brown had always been a winning coach, starting with his days in Massillon, Ohio, where he grew up. After playing quarterback in high school and college, Brown returned to Massillon High School to coach his alma mater to 80 wins in nine years, including a 58–1–0 record at one stretch.

At the age of thirty-two, Brown received a call from Ohio State University. Fourteen years earlier, that school had declared him too small to try out for its football team. Now it wanted him as the coach. Brown accepted but still had trouble getting onto the football field. Before his first game, he was not allowed past the stadium entrance, because he did not have a ticket. He had to toss pebbles at the locker room window to get his players' attention so they could let him in. Everyone knew him by his second season, as he led the Buckeyes to the national title.

In 1946, the AAFC's first season, Brown assembled a team of smart players who could understand his complicated system. He even used intelligence tests to measure the players' learning ability. Brown's teams breezed past opponents with a quick passing game that could pick holes in any defense. Upon joining the NFL in 1950, the Browns won divisional titles their first six years.

Brown had only one losing season in his seventeen years as coach when new owner Art Modell fired him in 1962. "I walked out of the stadium and got into my car as if in a dream," Brown recalled. "I couldn't believe what had just happened."[2]

After five years away from the game, Brown built another team from scratch—the new Cincinnati Bengals. He recruited more smart players, and the Bengals reached the playoffs in their third year. In 1975, Brown coached the Bengals to an 11–3 record, then retired. In forty-five years of coaching, he was considered the hardest worker of his time, but he didn't see it that way. "I never worked a day in my life," he said, "because what I did wasn't work—it was fun."[3]

PAUL BROWN

BORN: September 7, 1908, Norwalk, Ohio.

DIED: August 5, 1996.

HIGH SCHOOL: Massillon High School, Massillon, Ohio.

COLLEGE: Miami University of Ohio.

PRO: Cleveland Browns, 1946–1962; Cincinnati Bengals, 1968–1973.

HONORS: Pro Football Hall of Fame, 1967.

After his career with Cleveland was over, Paul Brown quickly turned the newly formed Cincinnati Bengals into a winning team. Brown was inducted into the Pro Football Hall of Fame in 1967.

JOE GIBBS

Joe Gibbs took over as head coach of the Washington Redskins in 1980. After the 1982 season, Gibbs was named NFC Coach of the Year for leading the Redskins to their first Super Bowl victory.

IF IT WEREN'T FOR A BLOWN ENGINE, Joe Gibbs might never have become a football coach. He had just finished playing college football at San Diego State University in 1963, and he was more interested in drag racing than in anything else. He cruised the San Diego hot spots in his '33 Ford, always looking for a race with another dragster. But when his engine exploded one day and he didn't have the money to fix it, he accepted a job as an assistant coach with San Diego State University. The NFL, and especially the Washington Redskins, should be grateful for that blown engine.

Gibbs became the first coach in NFL history to win three Super Bowls with three different quarterbacks. When he retired after the 1992 season, he had amassed 140 victories in just twelve seasons. He could have coached much longer, but he wanted to return to his other passion—auto racing.

Gibbs had the good fortune to work as an assistant coach under three highly successful coaches: Don Coryell at San Diego State, John McKay at the University of Southern California, and Frank Broyles at the University of Arkansas. "Every year was a learning experience for me," Gibbs said.

He took what he had learned to the pro level when he coached with Coryell again, this time for the San Diego Chargers. Together they got the Chargers flying high. In 1980, the Redskins decided they needed a new head coach. General Manager Bobby Beathard reached for Gibbs.

Gibbs's first team started terribly, losing its first five games. "I began to think I would be the only coach who was fired before winning even one game," he said.[1] Then, the

Redskins rebounded to win 8 of their last 11. The next year they won it all.

With mobile Joe Theismann at quarterback, the Redskins rolled through the strike-shortened 1982 season with an 8–1 record, then beat three teams in the playoffs to reach the Super Bowl. In the title game, Gibbs's innovative one-back offense, with John Riggins plowing the ball forward, wore down the Dolphins. The Redskins came from behind in the fourth quarter to win, 27–17.

In 1988, Gibbs's Redskins won the Super Bowl again, this time relying on the strong arm of quarterback Doug Williams. Washington torched the Denver Broncos for 5 touchdowns in the second quarter and won easily, 42–10.

In 1992, Gibbs made history by earning his third Super Bowl triumph with a different quarterback, as steady Mark Rypien guided the Redskins to a 37–24 win over the Buffalo Bills. After the season, Gibbs retired.

Gibbs's intense work habits set him apart. When he wasn't on the practice field with his team, he was usually in the Redskins coaches' office, watching game films. Most weeknights, he slept in the office, often not going to sleep until dawn. "Joe coached 'till he dropped," said Redskins general manager Charley Casserly. "He literally gave us every ounce he had."[2]

Since retiring in 1993, Gibbs has become a television football analyst, a motivational speaker, and a volunteer counselor for at-risk teenagers. He also has become an owner of an auto-racing team. In his first year, his car won the Daytona 500, racing's equivalent to the Super Bowl.

"Most people get to experience one dream in their lifetime if they're lucky," Gibbs said. "I had football for twenty-nine years. Now I get to go drag racing."[3]

JOE GIBBS

BORN: November 25, 1940, Mocksville, North Carolina.

HIGH SCHOOL: Santa Fe Springs High School, San Diego, California.

COLLEGE: Cerritos (Calif.) Junior College; San Diego State University.

PRO: Washington Redskins, 1981–1992.

HONORS: Pro Football Hall of Fame, 1996.

Concentrating on the game, Joe Gibbs studies the action on the field. Gibbs led the Washington Redskins to three Super Bowl wins.

Bud Grant

The Temperature Was Below Freezing. The field at Metropolitan Stadium in Bloomington, Minnesota, was covered with snow. Bud Grant stood on the Vikings' sideline with his arms folded across his chest. He didn't look cold. He didn't act cold.

The Vikings were locked in a bitter struggle with the Los Angeles Rams for the 1974 NFC championship. Many of the Rams were gathered around the heaters on their sideline, trying to keep warm. Not the Vikings. They stood along their sideline with their coach, staring out at the field. They weren't huddled around their heaters for one simple reason—there were no heaters on the Vikings sideline. Grant never allowed it.

"I don't want players to look forward to being warm," Grant explained. "Their attention should be on the field, not worrying about where the heater is."[1]

Such strategy usually worked for the Vikings, and it worked on this wintry day, too. With quarterback Fran Tarkenton directing the offense, and Carl Eller and Alan Page leading the Purple People Eaters' defense, the Vikings beat the Rams, 14–10, to win the title.

In many ways, Grant's approach to the game was different from that of the other coaches. He didn't like training camp, so he started camp each year just one week before the first preseason game. He had rules about what and when each player could eat. At one practice, he spent thirty minutes coaching them to stand properly at attention for the national anthem. He was so odd that his players called him Spaceman.

Bud Grant coaches the Minnesota Vikings through a practice session.

BUD GRANT

Grant had another nickname, too. During games, his expression never changed. He always looked serious, so his players called him Old Stone Face. The truth was, Grant was quite emotional inside; he just didn't want to show it. He figured that if he kept his cool, his players would do the same.

Grant's real first name was Harold, but that was also his father's name. His mother began calling him Buddy Boy, and the name stuck. As a boy, Grant contracted polio, which left his left leg shorter than his right. Doctors said exercise would be a cure, so Grant began playing sports. He became so good at football and basketball that he played in high school, in college, and professionally. He played basketball for two years with the Minneapolis Lakers, then concentrated solely on football. He played receiver for the Philadelphia Eagles, then for the Winnipeg Blue Bombers of the Canadian Football League, where he became head coach in 1957, at the young age of twenty-nine. In the next decade, he led the Blue Bombers to victory in four Grey Cups, the Canadian equivalent of the Super Bowl.

Likewise, with the Vikings, Grant led his team to four Super Bowls in the 1970s. Only this time, he lost all four games. Those losses tainted a brilliant career that ended in 1985, when Grant retired from coaching to pursue his favorite hobbies, including hunting and fishing. Football fans in Minnesota still remember him as the soft-spoken coach with the odd coaching methods, who made opponents shiver at the thought of playing the Vikings.

BUD GRANT

BORN: May 20, 1927, Superior, Wisconsin.

HIGH SCHOOL: Superior Central High School, Superior, Wisconsin.

COLLEGE: University of Minnesota.

PRO: Winnipeg Blue Bombers (CFL), 1957–1966; Minnesota
Vikings, 1967–1983, 1985.

PRO PLAYER: Philadelphia Eagles, 1951–1952; Winnipeg Blue
Bombers, 1953–1956.

HONORS: Pro Football Hall of Fame, 1994.

Bud Grant guided the Vikings to four Super Bowls. Grant was
enshrined in the Pro Football Hall of Fame in 1994.

GEORGE HALAS

GEORGE HALAS SWUNG HARD and whacked Rube Marquard's pitch to the wall in center. Halas, the rookie right fielder for the New York Yankees, had an easy double. But Halas was aggressive. He tried to stretch it into a triple. The Brooklyn Dodgers relayed the throw to third. Halas slid hard. Out! Not only that, Halas suffered a hip injury. He was sent to the minors and never made it back to the big leagues. The Yankees' right fielder the following year was Babe Ruth.

Ruth became a baseball legend; but Halas became famous in another sport—football. Halas founded the Chicago Bears and helped create the National Football League.

Halas grew up in a poor family. As a boy he worked as a janitor to help support the family. He played football in high school, but he weighed only 140 pounds, so a future in pro football seemed unlikely. At the University of Illinois, he tried out as a halfback. When the coach saw his aggressiveness, he said, "He runs so hard, he is likely to kill himself. Better make him an end."[1]

After graduating in 1919, Halas became the right fielder for the Yankees, but he soon lost his starting spot to the injury and Ruth. While he was recovering, A. E. Staley, owner of a corn products company in Decatur, Illinois, hired him to organize a football team that would represent the company. Halas recruited athletes from the area and formed the Decatur Staleys.

On September 17, 1920, Halas met with ten other men representing football clubs. The meeting took place in an automobile showroom in Canton, Ohio. "There were no chairs," Halas recalled. "We lounged around on fenders and

GEORGE HALAS

Legendary coach George Halas helped create the National Football League.

running boards and talked things over."[2] That day, Halas and the other men formed the American Professional Football Association.

Halas was head coach and played left end for the Staleys. He earned the largest salary on the team—$100 a game. Decatur beat the Moline Tractors, 20–0, in its first game. On ten occasions, the Staleys shut out their opponents on their way to a 10–1–2 record. The next year, Halas was given part ownership of the team. He moved the Staleys to Chicago, where they played at Wrigley Field (then called Cubs Park) and lost just once again. In 1922, Halas changed the team's name to the Chicago Bears. Then he convinced the league to change its name to the National Football League.

In 1925, Halas persuaded legendary superback Red Grange of the University of Illinois to join the Bears. Grange made his professional debut with the Bears less than a week after playing his final college game. Halas decided to promote the NFL by showing off his new superstar on a hectic tour—playing eight games, in eight different cities, in a twelve-day stretch. The Bears won their first four games, but grew weary and lost their last four. They finished the tour against the Giants in New York, where a record crowd of nearly eighty thousand fans turned out to watch. Halas's plan had worked.

Through the 1930s and 1940s, the NFL continued to grow, and Halas contributed in many ways. His Bears were the first to use assistant coaches, hold daily practices, scout opponents on film, use a band to entertain fans at halftime, and broadcast games on radio. His teams in the 1940s played with such fervor that they earned the nickname Monsters of the Midway. Halas retired in 1968 because of arthritis. By then, "Papa Bear" had amassed 324 victories and 6 championships.

GEORGE HALAS

BORN: February 2, 1895, Chicago, Illinois.

DIED: October 31, 1983.

HIGH SCHOOL: Crane High School, Chicago, Illinois.

COLLEGE: University of Illinois.

PRO: Chicago Bears, 1920–1929, 1933–1942, 1946–1955, 1958–1967.

HONORS: Pro Football Hall of Fame, 1963.

Halas currently ranks second all-time in coaching victories. He led the Bears to six league championships during his coaching tenure.

JIMMY JOHNSON

JIMMY JOHNSON HAD A DECISION TO MAKE. Four minutes remained in the Cowboy's 1992 NFC championship game against San Francisco. Johnson's Dallas Cowboys led the 49ers, 24–20. The Cowboys had the ball at their own 21-yard line. Most coaches would be conservative and call a running play or a short pass. Johnson called for a bomb.

Quarterback Troy Aikman surprised the 49ers by dropping back to throw. Receiver Alvin Harper flashed across the field. Aikman hit him with a perfect spiral, and Harper raced 70 yards to set up the clinching touchdown. The Cowboys won, 30–20, to reach the Super Bowl.

"How 'bout them Cowboys!" Johnson shouted in the locker room.[1] He had every reason to be thrilled. He had replaced the immortal Tom Landry four years earlier and turned the Cowboys from losers to winners.

Four years later, Johnson was at it again. In January 1996, the great Don Shula retired from the Miami Dolphins, and Johnson stepped in. It isn't easy to replace a legend. Johnson has done it twice.

Johnson has always been a tireless worker. In high school, he played every down on offense and defense as a lineman. He became an All-Conference defensive lineman at the University of Arkansas, and he led the Razorbacks to the 1964 national championship.

For the next fourteen years, Johnson learned plenty about coaching as an assistant coach at Louisiana Tech University, Wichita State University, Iowa State University, the University of Oklahoma, the University of Arkansas, and the University of Pittsburgh.

JIMMY JOHNSON

After leading the University of Miami Hurricanes and the Dallas Cowboys to championships, Jimmy Johnson took over for Don Shula as head coach of the Miami Dolphins.

In 1979, he took over a losing Oklahoma State University program and led it to two bowl games. He gained fame at the University of Miami, where he led the Hurricanes to the 1987 national championship. During one stretch, the Hurricanes won 36 straight regular-season games.

When Landry was fired by new Cowboys owner Jerry Jones early in 1989, and replaced by Johnson, critics called it a big mistake. One newspaper columnist wrote, "It's as if the rustlers just shot John Wayne."[2] Johnson had to overcome heavy media criticism—and a bad team.

When Johnson first assembled his new Dallas team in minicamp, he couldn't believe how awful they were. He thought even his University of Miami team had more talent. "The Hurricanes could have beaten the Cowboys, and beaten them bad," he said.[3]

Just as Johnson thought, the Cowboys were bad, going 1–15 that first year. But Johnson carefully built a new team through the college draft, picking players like Aikman and running back Emmitt Smith. Dallas won 7 games in 1990, then reached the playoffs the next year. In 1992, the Cowboys won it all, routing the Buffalo Bills, 52–17, in the Super Bowl. Johnson had become the first coach ever to win both the college national championship and the Super Bowl. In 1993, he did it again, beating the Bills in the Super Bowl, this time by a 30–13 score. Then, at the very top of his career, he quit the Cowboys.

Johnson was not done with coaching. After being a television football analyst for two years, he replaced Shula as coach at Miami. Anytime now, Johnson may be heard saying, "How 'bout them Dolphins!"

JIMMY JOHNSON

BORN: July 16, 1943, Port Arthur, Texas.

HIGH SCHOOL: Jefferson High School, Port Arthur, Texas.

COLLEGE: University of Arkansas.

PRO: Dallas Cowboys, 1989–1993; Miami Dolphins, 1996– .

HONORS: Associated Press NFL Coach of the Year, 1990.

Focusing on the task at hand, Jimmy Johnson plans his next move.

CURLY LAMBEAU

THERE ARE THIRTY TEAMS IN THE NFL, but only one plays in a small town and is owned by its fans—the Green Bay Packers. The man responsible for this is Earl "Curly" Lambeau, the team's founder in 1919, its earliest star, and its coach for the first thirty-one years.

Lambeau and his rival, George Halas, were football's pioneers, coaching in an era when sandlot teams staged reckless brawls in the dirt or mud or snow. In today's world of indoor stadiums with artificial turf and controlled temperatures, the Packers still play at an outdoor stadium in Wisconsin that features those brutal cold elements of long ago. The stadium is Lambeau Field, named after the legendary coach whose lifetime passion was football.

During his first season of competitive football in the eighth grade, Lambeau suffered a broken ankle. He refused to quit the game, however, and it turned out to be his only major injury in a long career. He went on to star as a running back in high school, and then joined the great George Gipp in the backfield at Notre Dame, where he learned briefly under college coaching wizard Knute Rockne.

After his freshman season at Notre Dame, Lambeau contracted a tonsil infection that grew so serious he had to drop out of school. Once recovered, he took a job for low wages at the Indian Packing Company, a meatpacking factory. A year later, the company decided to sponsor a football team. The team's name would be the Packers. Lambeau was asked to serve as halfback and quarterback, team captain, and coach.

CURLY LAMBEAU

Legendary coach Curly Lambeau draws up a play as one of his players looks on to learn what he is supposed to do.

Lambeau held three practice sessions a week and taught his players some of the skills and strategies he had learned from Rockne at Notre Dame. The team could not afford the best equipment and had to make do, using magazines as shin guards. The Packers played 11 games their first year and won 10 of them. In an early-season game, three of Lambeau's players suffered injuries on running plays. "So we just passed them silly and won 33–0," he said. "That was the day I realized how valuable the forward pass could be."[1] From then on, instead of pounding his lightly padded running backs into the line as other teams did, and risk injury, Lambeau devised a safer offense built on passing the ball.

After another winning season in 1920, Lambeau's team joined the newly formed National Football League in 1921. The Packers were kicked out of the league following their first season as a result of using college players who played under phony names. Lambeau apologized to the league and pleaded for a second chance. The NFL granted it. Attendance at games in frigid Wisconsin was low in the early years, and to help support the team, Lambeau led fund-raising drives. Residents of Green Bay donated money, and that is why the Packers today are owned by the entire town.

Lambeau's final year as a player in 1929 ended with the team's first NFL title, and he coached the team to championships again the next two years. Lambeau resigned from the Packers in 1950, then coached the Chicago Cardinals and Washington Redskins each for two years without much success. It was obvious he had left his heart in Green Bay— right where it belonged.

Curly Lambeau

BORN: April 9, 1898, Green Bay, Wisconsin.

DIED: June 1, 1965.

HIGH SCHOOL: East High School, Green Bay, Wisconsin.

COLLEGE: University of Notre Dame.

PRO: Green Bay Packers, 1919–1949; Chicago Cardinals, 1950–1951; Washington Redskins, 1952–1953.

HONORS: Pro Football Hall of Fame, 1963.

Lambeau led the Green Bay Packers to six league championships. He was inducted into the Pro Football Hall of Fame in 1963—its first year of existence.

TOM LANDRY

Conferring with his coaches in the stands, Tom Landry
tries to decide the best course of action.

TOM LANDRY

TOM LANDRY KNEW RIGHT AWAY that he was in trouble. The expansion Dallas Cowboys of 1960 had just been created with rejects from other NFL teams. The worst three players from each team had been sent to Dallas. Landry was asked to coach them. When Landry got his first look at the motley squad, he had one thought. "It was just a matter of time," Landry said, "before I'd be fired."[1]

Even after Dallas went winless its first season, even after the Cowboys had losing seasons their next three years, Landry was not fired. In fact, after Landry's third losing season, he was given a new ten-year contract. The Dallas owners knew Landry was a coaching wizard. They figured the wins would eventually come. They were right.

Landry knew plenty about the game. He had played fullback and defensive back in high school, and those same positions at the University of Texas. His college years were interrupted by World War II, however, when he felt a duty to join the Air Force. He flew thirty missions in Europe. One time his plane was forced down, but he luckily managed to escape harm.

After returning to college to earn an engineering degree, Landry joined the New York Yankees of the AAFC as a defensive back. The next year, he joined the New York Giants of the NFL. He was not a fast runner, however. He found that the wide receivers in the NFL were far swifter than he was, and he struggled to keep up. He soon realized he had to outsmart them. He learned their moves by studying game films for hours every night. By game day, he knew every play and pass route of his opponent. He recognized plays at the line of scrimmage and barked them to his defensive teammates. Most of the time he was right. It was like having another coach on the field.

Landry learned so much about opposing offenses that he became the Giants' defensive coordinator in 1954, while he was still a player. During games, he coached his teammates on the sideline, then ran out to the field with them to stop the other team. Two years later, he quit playing so he could concentrate fully on coaching.

Defenses in the 1950s used six defensive linemen and a single linebacker. Landry created the 4-3-4 defense, with three linebackers given the freedom to blitz the quarterback or cover receivers. Within a few years, every team in the league was copying Landry's defense, so he created newer defenses to outfox them again. Defensive end Andy Robustelli said, "No matter what the opposition did, Tom always seemed to be just one step ahead of them."[2]

After Landry became head coach of the Cowboys and his team started winning, it didn't stop. Dallas reached the NFL title game in 1966 and 1967, then played in its first Super Bowl in 1971, barely losing to the Baltimore Colts. The Cowboys returned to the Super Bowl the following year, and this time Landry's team celebrated. Led by its Doomsday Defense, the Cowboys stuffed the Miami Dolphins, 24–3, in Super Bowl VI.

By now, Landry was using computers to design complicated offensive plays. He always seemed to push the right buttons, leading the Cowboys to the Super Bowl five times in the 1970s, winning in 1972 and in 1978. His teams continued their winning tradition through the 1980s. Through it all, Landry always remained calm on the sideline, dressed neatly in his suit, tie, and hat. He explained his cool appearance, saying, "When I see a great play, I can't cheer it. I'm a couple of plays ahead, just thinking."[3]

Tom Landry

BORN: September 11, 1924, Mission, Texas.

HIGH SCHOOL: Mission High School, Mission, Texas.

COLLEGE: University of Texas.

PRO: Dallas Cowboys, 1960–1988.

PRO PLAYER: New York Yankees, 1949; New York Giants, 1950–1955.

HONORS: Pro Football Hall of Fame, 1990.

Landry led the Cowboys to five Super Bowls, winning two of them.

VINCE LOMBARDI

Vince Lombardi had a great ability to motivate his players. In 1959, Lombardi was named the NFL Coach of the Year.

VINCE LOMBARDI

THE 1958 GREEN BAY PACKERS WERE LOSERS. They had won just one game all year, their tenth straight season with a losing record. A new coach was needed. The Packers reached for Vince Lombardi.

Lombardi was the tough-minded assistant coach of the New York Giants. The day he arrived in Green Bay, he showed just how demanding he was. He announced to club officials, "I want it understood that I am in complete command here."[1] Then he told his players, "I have never been on a losing team, gentlemen, and I do not intend to start now."[2]

Even as a boy, Lombardi was in charge. He was the oldest child in a strict home in Brooklyn, New York, and he gave the orders to the younger children. He played fullback in high school, then offensive guard at Fordham University, where he was one of the famed Seven Blocks of Granite.

He gained a reputation as a fiery coach at St. Cecilia High School in Englewood, New Jersey, growling like a bear at his players to fire them up. He used tricks to convince them that they were better than their opponents. Before a game against powerful rival Brooklyn Prep, he gave each of his players a pill that he said would make them bigger and stronger. The players believed him. St. Cecilia won, 6–0. The pills were made of sugar.

After leading St. Cecilia to six state championships in eight years, Lombardi returned to Fordham University as an assistant coach, where he perfected the T-formation offense. He assisted at Army, then the Giants, before the Packers came calling.

The Green Bay players realized right away that Lombardi meant business. He drilled them hard in practices, and screamed at them when they made a mistake. Barely 5-foot-8, he was much shorter than most of his players, but they feared him just the same. Huge tackle Henry Jordan admitted, "When he says sit down, I don't even look for a chair."[3]

Lombardi demanded winning, and that's just what he got. The Packers never had a losing season while he was coach. He taught flashy halfback Paul Hornung to be a hard-nosed runner. He transformed soft-spoken quarterback Bart Starr into a fierce leader. The Packers won the conference championship in Lombardi's second year, then lost the NFL title to the Philadelphia Eagles. It was the only playoff game Lombardi ever lost. In the title game the following season, the Packers crushed the Giants, 37–0.

In 1966, Lombardi's Packers won the first Super Bowl ever played, beating the Kansas City Chiefs, 35–10. They won Super Bowl II as well, beating the Oakland Raiders, 33–14. Lombardi's teams won five NFL championships and two Super Bowls in the 1960s, and Green Bay became known as Titletown USA. Lombardi wasn't satisfied, saying, "We never won as many as I wanted, which was all of them."[4]

Lombardi left the Packers after his second Super Bowl win to transform another losing team—the Washington Redskins—into a winner. But after engineering a winning season in his first year there, Lombardi fell ill. He died of cancer a few months later.

Throughout professional football there are reminders of Lombardi. The Green Bay Packer Hall of Fame is on Lombardi Avenue. Even the Super Bowl trophy that goes to the winning team is called the Lombardi Trophy. Lombardi's coaching career was cut short, but his memory lives on.

VINCE LOMBARDI

BORN: June 11, 1913, Brooklyn, New York.

DIED: September 3, 1970.

HIGH SCHOOL: St. Francis Prep High School, Brooklyn, New York.

COLLEGE: Fordham University.

PRO: Green Bay Packers, 1959–1967; Washington Redskins, 1969.

HONORS: Pro Football Hall of Fame, 1971.

Vince Lombardi's Packers won five NFL championships, including the first two Super Bowls.

DON SHULA

While coaching the Colts and the Dolphins, Don Shula reached the Super Bowl six times.

DON SHULA WAS IN THE MIDDLE of the field, shaking hands with his opponents, when Baltimore Colts owner Carroll Rosenbloom approached him. The Detroit Lions and Baltimore Colts had just completed a game near the end of the 1962 season. Shula was a young assistant coach for the Lions. What did Rosenbloom want with him?

"Are you ready to become a head coach?" the owner asked.

Shula was surprised at the question. But he remained calm, thought for a moment, and then answered. "The only way that you'll ever be able to find out," he said, "is to hire me and let me show you that I am capable of being a winner."[1]

Rosenbloom hired Shula three weeks later. It was a smart move. With the Colts and then with the Miami Dolphins, Shula went on to become the winningest coach in NFL history.

Shula is widely considered to be among the most honest coaches ever, but it was an act of dishonesty that kept him in football. He had just started playing the sport in high school when he came home one day with a gash across his nose. When his parents saw the injury, they refused to let him play again. Shula wanted to play so badly that he forged his parents' signatures on a permission slip and continued playing anyway. When his parents found out, he talked them into attending a game. They agreed, and saw their son return a punt 75 yards for a touchdown. They were instant football fans.

In 1951, Shula became one of only two rookies on Paul Brown's defending NFL champion Cleveland Browns. Shula peppered Brown with questions, wanting to learn all he could from the coach. Two years later, Shula was traded to the Baltimore Colts as part of the biggest deal in NFL history—a swap of fifteen players. Linebackers usually call defensive signals, but Shula understood strategy so well that he called signals for Baltimore from his cornerback position.

Shula's playing career ended in 1957 as a member of the Washington Redskins. He spent the next seven years as an assistant. Then, at the age of thirty-three, he was asked to return to the Colts as head coach.

The Colts were winners right away under Shula. In his seven years with Baltimore, his teams won 73 games and lost only 26.

The Miami Dolphins had won just 15 games in four years when Shula arrived in 1970, but he made them instantly competitive, winning 10 games. "Don Shula is competitive in everything," said assistant coach Monte Clark. "He's competitive eating breakfast."[2]

In Shula's second year, the Dolphins won the AFC Championship to reach Super Bowl VI. After losing to the Dallas Cowboys, the Dolphins vowed to return. Then came the miracle year of 1972. Shula's team swept through the season undefeated. They beat the Cleveland Browns and Pittsburgh Steelers in the playoffs, then defeated the Redskins, 14–7, in the Super Bowl. Shula's Dolphins had become the first team to go undefeated through 17 games in a season. They won the Super Bowl again the next year, and before Shula retired in 1995, they had reached the title game twice more.

"If I'm remembered for anything as a coach," Shula said, "I hope it's for playing within the rules. I also hope it will be said that my teams showed class and dignity in victory or defeat."[3]

Most of the time, it was in victory.

DON SHULA

BORN: January 4, 1930, Grand River, Ohio.

HIGH SCHOOL: Harvey High School, Painesville, Ohio.

COLLEGE: John Carroll University, Cleveland, Ohio.

PRO: Baltimore Colts, 1963–1969; Miami Dolphins, 1970–1995.

PRO PLAYER: Cleveland Browns, 1951–1953; Baltimore Colts, 1953–1956; Washington Redskins, 1957.

HONORS: Pro Football Hall of Fame, 1997.

Shula retired from coaching in 1996, winning a record 328 regular-season games.

BILL WALSH

IN 1978, THE SAN FRANCISCO 49ERS were the joke of the NFL. They had been led by six different head coaches in the previous five years. They had just finished a miserable 2–14 season—worst in the league. They would have had the very first pick in the college draft, but they had already traded it away.

It would take a genius to turn things around. Bill Walsh was asked to try. "I had to try to put together a respectable team from the ruins," said Walsh, who was hired as head coach in 1979.[1] Three years later, the 49ers were Super Bowl champions. When Walsh retired following the 1988 season, the 49ers had won three Super Bowls and been named Team of the Decade. Walsh was declared a genius.

Walsh's success was no surprise. He was a master craftsman as an assistant coach wherever he went, turning quarterbacks into Hall of Famers. Walsh had played quarterback himself in high school, but a series of injuries in college cut short his playing career. He worked his way up the coaching ladder, first as head coach at Washington High School in Fremont, California, then as an assistant at Stanford University and the University of California, and finally as the Oakland Raiders' running backs coach.

In 1968, Walsh joined the Cincinnati Bengals as passing coach. He turned Ken Anderson into the top-ranked quarterback in the league by 1974. In 1976, Walsh moved to the San Diego Chargers, where he transformed Dan Fouts into a "Top Gun" quarterback.

Two years later, the 49ers called, and Walsh went right to work. In three years he drafted almost a whole new team,

Bill Walsh was known for having a great offensive mind when the San Francisco 49ers hired him to be their head coach in 1978.

BILL WALSH

including Quarterback Joe Montana and Wide Receiver Dwight Clark. That duo teamed up to make The Catch, which changed 49er fortunes for good. In the 1981 NFC title game against mighty Dallas at San Francisco's Candlestick Park, Clark caught a last-minute pass from Montana in the back of the end zone to win, 28–27. Two weeks later, Walsh was leading his team out the tunnel for Super Bowl XVI against the Bengals. "The excitement, the intensity is unbelievable," Walsh remembered. "Eighty thousand people roaring in anticipation. You're not even sure you can think straight."[2] Walsh kept his wits about him and coached his team to a 26–21 victory.

Walsh liked to have fun with his players. Before the Super Bowl, for instance, he dressed up as a bellhop and helped carry his players' bags into the hotel. Someone finally recognized him, and everyone had a big laugh.

Walsh was especially known for his West Coast Offense and for his knack in scripting plays. The West Coast Offense features a passing scheme in which running backs are as much a threat to catch the ball as are the receivers. Many NFL teams still use Walsh's offense today. One of Walsh's routines was to script, or plan, the first twenty-five plays of each game. The script might start with a sweep, then a screen pass, then a draw play, then a bomb. The 49ers would rehearse these twenty-five plays, in order, over and over again in practice until they were executed perfectly, then use them in that order in the game. The strategy usually worked.

Walsh's teams were playoff contenders every year, and the 49ers won two more Super Bowls, in 1985 over the Miami Dolphins and in 1989 over the Bengals again. After his team's third Super Bowl triumph, Walsh stepped aside as coach.

BILL WALSH

BORN: November 30, 1931, Los Angeles, California.

HIGH SCHOOL: Hayward High School, Hayward, California.

COLLEGE: San Mateo Junior College; San Jose State University.

PRO: San Francisco 49ers, 1979–1988.

HONORS: Pro Football Hall of Fame, 1993.

Walsh led the 49ers to three Super Bowl victories. Today, his West Coast Offense is used by many professional and college coaches.

CHAPTER NOTES

Paul Brown

1. Denis J. Harrington, *The Pro Football Hall of Fame* (Jefferson, N.C.: McFarland & Co., 1991), p. 297.
2. Paul Brown, *PB: The Paul Brown Story* (New York: Atheneum, 1979), p. 282.
3. Ibid., p. 377.

Joe Gibbs

1. Pro Football Hall of Fame media notes.
2. Thomas George, "For Joe Gibbs, Greatest Pain Is in Leaving the Redskins," *The New York Times*, March 6, 1993, p. 29.
3. Rick Voegelin, "Gibbs Goes Straight: Former Redskins Coach Joe Gibbs Finds Fast Success in Drag Racing," *Sport*, July 1995, p. 19.

Bud Grant

1. Pro Football Hall of Fame media notes.

George Halas

1. Mac Davis, *100 Greatest Football Heroes* (New York: Grosset & Dunlap, 1973), p. 103.
2. Richard Whittingham, *The Chicago Bears* (New York: Simon & Schuster, 1986), p. 18.

Jimmy Johnson

1. Jimmy Johnson, *Turning the Thing Around* (New York: Hyperion, 1993), p. 241.
2. Ibid., p. 31.
3. Ibid., p. 35.

Curly Lambeau

1. Pro Football Hall of Fame media notes.

Tom Landry

1. Tom Landry, *Tom Landry—An Autobiography* (New York: HarperCollins, 1990), p. 127.
2. Denis J. Harrington, *The Pro Football Hall of Fame* (Jefferson, N.C.: McFarland & Co., 1991), p. 313.
3. Ian Thorne, *Meet the Coaches* (Mankato, Minn.: Creative Education, 1975), p. 24.

Vince Lombardi

1. Jim Doherty, "In Chilly Green Bay, Curly's Old Team Is Still Packing Them In," *Smithsonian*, August 1991, p. 85.

2. Pro Football Hall of Fame media notes.

3. Doherty, p. 85.

4. Ted Zalewski, *Vince Lombardi—He Is Still With Us* (Mankato, Minn.: Creative Education, 1974), p. 22.

Don Shula

1. Don Shula, *The Winning Edge* (New York: E. P. Dutton & Co., 1973), p. 85.

2. Hank Nuwer, *Strategies of the Great Football Coaches* (New York: Franklin Watts, 1988), p. 125.

3. Richard Whittingham, *Sunday Mayhem—A Celebration of Pro Football in America* (Dallas, Tex.: Taylor Publishing Co., 1987), p. 269.

Bill Walsh

1. Bill Walsh, *Building a Champion* (New York: St. Martin's Press, 1990), p. 55.

2. Ibid., p. 1.

INDEX